For the Love of Purple

Nailah Robinson

*Dedicated to my children,
Unique, Seyvon, and Karma.
May this work help you
understand your "crazy"
mother, and bring us closer
together.*

Table of Contents

***Insomniac**
Inspired By Wandering
Through Dreams
I Miss
The Toll of Time*

For the Love of Purple

For The Love Of Purple

Royalty
Blood deep
Just plum good
The smell of lavender fills the air
And I am transfixed into my happy place
Passion fruit fulfills my passion for life
My first true love
In all shades
Live purple
Live free
Let it rain over you
Like the luxury of love
That you shower over the world
The color that dreams were made of
Dark, yet beautiful
Just like my dark, yet beautiful soul
I am drawn to you
The unique underrated you
For the love of purple

My Voice

I am offering you my voice
Hold it gently with both hands
Be bold when you use it
Carry it with you always
For I love you
I need you to have all that I can give

My voice is my greatest strength
I have conditioned it to speak life
That is my gift to you
The words you can not find
Hide within
When you are stuck in your darkness
Let my voice be your lightest friend
When you are lost
Let my voice guide your way

I am offering you my voice
It is all that I have to give
Carry it with you always

But hold it gently with both hands

The Fire

I am the doorway to knowledge
I know all and I know nothing
I am the path to enlightenment
Seek and ye shall find me
I am the answer to all my needs
I am beyond the Phoenix
I am the fire

Where I'm From

I am from Alabama soil and Illinois
wind
All mixed together to make me
California strong
I am from fried chicken and collard
greens
Yams and sweet potato pies
I am from Willie Mae's crown and
Robert's plum trees
Effie's strength and Edwards tenacity
I am from swap meets and liquor
stores
Durant Square and Eastmont Mall
I am from poetry in motion
Hip hop and R&B
I am from step teams and childhood
dreams
I am from the middle and last leaf on
the branch
I am from the first sprout from the
new line
Never snapped
Never broken

For the Love of Unique

Unique

Undeniably my first true love
Never knew it could be like this
I looked into your eyes and in the
Quiet of your glance the
Universe suddenly made sense
Everything I am now is shaped by you

My first child
Light of my world
The dream come true
Unique

Quiet and Dark

I'm the only one awake
In this quiet darkness
Forced to listen to my own thoughts
It's enough to drive you insane
What's my name
Natalie
No, that's not it
Natasha
No
That's okay
Who needs a name
Not here
In this deep, dark, quiet place
Where you're the only one awake
Forced to listen to your own thoughts
Did that bill get paid
Yesterday
The laundry
Tomorrow
He suddenly snores softly next to me
And it would almost be a lullaby
Except the thoughts aren't done with
me yet

Did you remember to turn off the stove
Last night
Better go check that one
Do you smell gas
It's awfully hot
No
Nothing's on
Check on the children
So peaceful in their bed
Not a care in the world
To be young again
Suddenly a call
A very quiet whisper
Meant for just two
"Mom"
Oh right, that's my name

Soul Ties

The eyes are the window to the soul
But your touch is the door to my heart
The heat from your fingertips sets my
heart to flame
I try to resist, but it never comes fairly
to play
I know that you're no good for me
But my body craves more and more
I stare deeply into your eyes and see
The man that I've always dreamed for
Everyone knows the harm you've done
They tell me, "He's not the one"
But when you touch me, I can't hear
those calls
It's like a siren song, but not spoken
with the tongue
We'll never be left in peace, I fear
You've already made that bed
But our love is deeper than peace and war
And it'll last past we're both dead

For it burns through the children we've bred

Simplicity

There's beauty in simplicity
The silent elegance
Because the loud killed me
And I'll never let it kill me again
The peace beyond the storm compels me
And I slumber more than when I was a baby
The curiosity of simplicity
Sparks the flame of tranquility
And I feel right at home

My Sister's Keeper

Guilty by association
I am my sister's keeper
I keep their secrets and
Their secrets keep me
Be a cold day in Hell
Before I tell

Did you hear about Tammy
That man went upside her head again
Drinking and carrying on in sin
But I never told

And did you hear about Tracey
She let them kids run wild
Now she's pregnant with another child
That story still hasn't left my mouth

Did you hear about Monica
Stubborn to the end
Quit her job and lost all her friends
Kept my thoughts to myself and never
said a word

And Lacey
Now she's the one

Got three boyfriends
And still looking for one
But who told her husband?
I swear I wasn't the one

Innocence becomes me
As I hold their secrets without fail
Because I am my sister's keeper
I keep their secrets
And their secrets keep me

Raised On Hip Hop

Raise on hip hop
Draped in gold chains and bamboo
earrings
LL Cool J with his love rapping
Bopping my head to the beat
Never off key
NWA was my education
Run DMC voice of a generation

Raised on hip hop
Dr Dre the best physician
A dose of hits in my blood
Gave us Snoop, 50, and Slim Shady
Living my life in the best position

Raised on hip hop
Queen Latifah, MC Lyte,
Salt-N-Pepa, TLC
Taught me everything I needed to
know
About my femininity

Raised on hip hop
Wu Tang Clan taught me to be nothing
to fuck with

While Common made it all make sense
Slick Rick read me a bedtime story
While the Fresh Prince taught me how
to be me no matter where I reside

Raised on hip hop
Tupac and Biggie
Made our lines clear
Raised on hip hop
Everything I hold dear

Moving Mountains

Made to move mountains
We've been just strong enough
Moving inch by inch day by day
No mountain prove to be too tough

We are a resilient people
Doing what we have to do
To do what we want
And while doing it looking so cool
People want to be us so bad
But they could never handle these
problems
We were built for this life
We look at the problems and we solve
them

Lost so much
Gained so few
Couldn't begin to understand
Everything we've been through

But we were made to move mountains
We've always been just strong enough

'Cause we are a resilient people
And no mountain has ever been too tough

For the Love of Seyvon

Seyvon

Son
Even when you make me mad You
bring my life so much joy Very
protective of those you love
Ordinary could never describe you
Nor could I ever deny you

My baby
My headache
My heartache
My love

Forever and always
I am your mother
And you are my son

I write

In a feverish haze
I put pen to page
And I write

Waking every day
I think of something to say
And I write

When I start to feel crazed
The only way to change
Is when I write

When I feel a little rage
I give myself some aid
When I write

When I'm hurt and feeling jaded
I know just the way to play it
So I write

The Loop

He consumes me
His touch burns his name into my soul
I try to leave
But his spirit takes hold
I'm powerless
A simple whisper in my ear
I'm forever linked to him
And it's abundantly clear
I can't escape him
Try as I might
Our love was once blinding
But still I fight
I'm in the constant loop of emotion
Trying hard to break free
And yet my heart continues to melt

When he simply looks at me

Social

My grandma would love this
Can't play it cool no more
The wait is over
I'm no longer a child
It's in my blood to be a survivor
So I'm curious
How has another day gone by without
creativity
Freedom is your birthright
Passion is your calling
Let me give it to you straight
No chaser
There's a rumor going around
That's the end of the conversation

The River Dance

I dance with the river
Shaking and swaying with the rhythm
of the ripples
Gyrating to the splash on the banks
Don't go off somewhere else, dear
traveler
Move with me
Shake of the days dust into the wind
Let it carry us back from where we
began
Move with the pebbles beneath our
feet
Allow the water to splash upon us
Dance with the river now
Leave your stress in the ripples
For I used to be a traveler too
And they killed all of the pieces that
were the best of me
Now I dance with the river
Shaking and swaying with the rhythm
of the ripples
Gyrating to the splash on the banks
As I live, and live again

Sleepless

Am I keeping you awake with my
thoughts of you
I can't reach you, so that's
implausibly true
You've been gone too long
I'm no longer inspired
Yet I sit with this pen in my hand
And my soul on fire
I know you feel this energy; it can't
just be me
We are connected through more than
a touch
And our hearts were never set free
I was never heartbroken because you
never said goodbye
You just left one day
And I'll never know why
I ached for you, but I couldn't cry
So I'm going to sleep now, and you
can live with these thoughts
Cause having one more sleepless
night is something I will not

Til death do us part

I keep dreaming of your ghost
"Will you marry me,"
Playing through my mind on repeat
A broken record
The movie of out love
On rewind and replay
Rewind and replay
Rewind and replay
Wake up
Daydream of those moments
De ja vue
I hate you
You pull at my heartstrings
As it calls out
For a man who no longer
Calls out to me
It's so loud
It's deafening
Covers all the holes of my life
But stabs deep like a knife
Overwhelming passion
From which I'll never recover
Why can't I marry my mind to my

heart
My mind knows it's over
But my heart remembers
"Til death do us part"

<u>For the Love of Karma</u>

Karma

Keeping it real
All of the time
Remembering everything
My life was complete with you
And our family became whole

A leader in every way
My baby girl
A mind of her own
My mini me, only so bold

Descendents

I am the descendent of Shaka
kaSenzagakhona "Zulu"
I come from a line of kings and queens
I know my neighbors and they know me
We fight, we build, we create
And I will defend my right to survive in this
distant land to the end
Even to my "family and friends"
I may not make it
But for today…I live

I am the descendent of Kunta Kinte
I will always survive the waves and storms
But I will not sit by in complicity
I will get my freedom through life or death
Always fighting or running for something
more

I am the descendent of Nat Turner
Struggling for my freedom and the freedom
of my people
And they fear me as they should because they
now know what I am capable of
And they know who I am

But "Was not Christ crucified?"
Indeed he was and so am I
They will say I was crazy to soothe their
consciences
But we who know the struggle will
understand
They made me this way

I am the descendent of Harriet Tubman
Bringing others to freedom with me
Never forgetting those we've left behind
And always standing on truth

I am the descendent of Madam CJ Walker
I will make something out of nothing
And you will buy it
And you will love it
And I will laugh in the face of the privilege
that you have afforded me

I am the descendent of Martin Luther King Jr
and Malcolm X
I believe in peace
And I do have a dream
But I'm going to live free
By any means necessary

I am the descendent of Huey P Newton,
Bobby Seale, and Angela Davis
I wear my afro with pride
I put my fist in the air
Because all power does belong to the people
And the struggle is real

I went to school with Rodney King and
Latasha Harlins
We learned that the justice system did not
work for us
And we could not all just get along
This was never a country for the people by
the people
And until we understand that we are all
people, it never will be

Our teachers were Maya Angelou, Langston
Hughes, James Brown, Public Enemy, and
NWA
We shouted "We're Black and we're proud"
And "Fuck the police"
All in one breath
We felt pride in the fact that
We rise
And we fought the power
But we were still not free

I am the sister of Kalief Browder, Trayvon
Martin, Philando Castile, Alton Sterling,
Oscar Grant, Eric Garner, Michael Brown,
George Floyd
And the others to come
Say their name
I am my brothers' keeper
I throw my hands up and yell
"Hands up, Don't shoot"
I wear the banner "Black Lives Matter"
I am one, but there are many
I am tired
But I will not rest
And neither will the generations after me

Me

I am a good girl
With some bad girl tendencies
Don't fit in any box
So please don't try to check me
I am the enigma
Most don't understand
But a few moments with me
And you're putty in my hand
An extreme pacifist
But I'll protect my family and friends
And don't disturb my peace
For that I'll fight till the end
Most people think
I am simply what they see
But for those special quirky parts
You should really get to know me

Hummingbird

I am the hummingbird
I will not be here long
I'm may hover
But I am fast forward in flight
I am comfortable in high altitudes
And I am incredibly tuned in
Going from flower to flower
Helping in pollination
I cannot walk
I must fly
No other species can move like me I
see all the colors and they call to me
I will stop by your feeder, but don't
you dare touch mine
They are fascinated by my song
But I will not be here long
I am the hummingbird

Invisibility

I love my invisibility
That's where I'm truly me
I'm comfortable in the shadows
I've never wanted to be the star of the
show
I don't know how to stand in the light
But I take my cues from others who
might
Play my part for a little while
Stand here, look pretty, and don't
forget to smile
But I'm uncomfortable with being
seen
And I love my superpower
Invisibility

Insomniac

Wide awake
It's getting late
Maybe some TV
Nothing I want to see
A good book
Nothing worth the look
A calming song
Everything's all wrong
Maybe some loving
Ugh...nope...nothing
Trying some food
I'm not in the mood
Something to drink
Pouring it out in the sink
Maybe if I clean
God, I just want to dream
Playing games on my phone
Battery died, it's no longer on
Tomorrow I'll feel sick
All because tonight I'm
Insomniac

Inspired By Wandering
Through Dreams

There's stars in her eyes
Clear as day
Hair flowing in the wind
Crown banged and bruised
Barely recognizable
But still there
She hugs herself
Nobody else has remember to do it
She was beautiful
Until the world beat her into
submission
The fire has gone
But the stars remain
Hope is a stranger she used to know
Life has taught her the hard lessons
She now sees the world for what it is
Poison coursing through her body
On its own treasure hunt
And yet she smiles
Through all that was broken
She has survived

I Miss

I really miss the illusion of you
That you shattered when you walked
away

That dream of who I thought you were
When I just knew that you were forever
stay

I missed that piece of you
That loved me so perfectly

I miss that picture of you
That seems so pure and sweet

I really miss that image of you
That had my brain craving more and
more

But I'll never miss the man before me
The veil has lifted, smoke cleared
That's not him anymore

The Toll of Time

I'm questioning all of my relationships lately
None of them mean the same thing
The people who were once my whole world...
Well I'm no longer eighteen
I thought I knew
Just what I wanted my life to be
I feel I'm all grown up now
Those things no longer serve me
I'm questioning all of my relationships
I would have never thought this to be true
Nothing feels the same anymore
Including my feelings for you

<u>Note from the Poet</u>

This book came from the need to reawaken my creativity. I found myself too busy to write anything, let alone poetry which takes more imagination and vision than I had time for. Poetry has always been my first love in writing. I find it moving in ways unimaginable, and I also love the way we can all interpret the same images in a different way, and we are all correct. It no longer matters what the poet meant when writing it, it only matters what the reader sees when they read it. I love that give and take dynamic.

I stumbled upon the 21 day challenge just when I was starting to feel a bit lost, and I knew I had to go for it. Writing 21 poems in 21 days, was exactly what I needed to shake things loose enough to get back into the writing mindset. Though these aren't my best pieces, these are the pieces that I needed to complete the whole puzzle that was becoming my life. This is the final product of that challenge. I added a few more that I wrote during this time also. It was as though, once I got started, I couldn't stop. This is the piece of me that I never want to lose again.

<u>About the Poet</u>

Nailah Robinson was born January 7, 1983. She is a wife and mother of 3. She currently teaches English Language Arts and Creative Writing in Phoenix, AZ.